The Sketchbook Kit

AN ARTIST'S GUIDE TO MATERIALS,
TECHNIQUES, AND PROJECTS

The Sketchbook Kit

AN ARTIST'S GUIDE TO MATERIALS, TECHNIQUES, AND PROJECTS

Text by
ANGELA GAIR

Illustrations by
ANTHONY COLBERT

CHRONICLE BOOKS
SAN FRANCISCO

First Published in the United States in 2001 by Chronicle Books

Text © 2001 The Ivy Press Limited
Illustrations © 2001 Anthony Colbert

ISBN-10 0-8118-3149-3
ISBN-13 978-0-8118-3149-9

Distributed in Canada by
Raincoast Books
9050 Shaughnessy Street
Vancouver, B.C. V6P 6E5

10 9 8

A CIP catalog record for this book is
available from the Library of Congress

This book was conceived, designed, and produced by
The Ivy Press Limited
The Old Candlemakers
Lewes, East Sussex BN7 2NZ

Art Director Peter Bridgewater
Publisher Sophie Collins
Editorial Director Steve Luck
Designer Clare Barber
Project Editor Caroline Earle
Picture Researcher Vanessa Fletcher

Chronicle Books LLC
85 Second Street
San Francisco, CA 94105
www.chroniclebooks.com

Printed in China by Winner Print and Packaging Ltd.

CONTENTS

KEEPING A SKETCHBOOK

If you are serious about painting and drawing, you should get into the habit of carrying a pocket-sized sketchbook with you everywhere and taking every opportunity to use it. Sketches don't have to be perfect, or even finished, and no one is judging you on the results. With a pencil and a sheet of paper you can catch life on the wing – a fleeting effect of light, a fascinating face, the graceful lines of your cat stretched out in the sun. Try to sketch something every day, no matter how small. There is no better way to improve your drawing skills and your powers of observation. Watching and absorbing subjects and recording them in your sketchbook will help you to "see" things with a fresh eye and to appreciate what you see far more deeply.

With practice you will be able to capture the likeness of friends and relatives.

Your sketchbook can be the seedbed of ideas for paintings or finished drawings; it can be the testing ground for compositional ideas and new ways of recording information; it can be the record book of your personal experiences. Above all, it is the place where you can enjoy the sheer pleasure of observing and recording something that you find beautiful.

Many artists find that sketching is such a pleasurable experience that it can become addictive! Over the years, you will probably build up quite a collection of sketchbooks and you will find them a rich source of inspiration and information. They become a record of your growth and development as an artist, and a fascinating visual diary of the places you have been and the people and things that have interested you. Browsing through them will give you great pleasure and many happy memories.

Pets and animals are challenging, but fascinating, subjects to draw.

7

MATERIALS FOR SKETCHING

One of the delights of sketching lies in the large and diverse range of materials that you can choose from. By experimenting with different media and papers, your sketches will remain fresh.

MONOCHROME MEDIA

Sketching is traditionally associated with pencil or pen, and it is surprising how much information you can convey in a simple monochrome drawing.

The humble graphite pencil is cheap, portable, versatile, and expressive.

PENCIL

Pencils come in several grades, from hard to soft. The best grades for sketching are an HB (in the middle of the range), which is good for general drawing, and a 6B (very soft), which gives a wide range of linear and tonal effects. There are also water-soluble pencils that can be wetted to create tonal washes.

Other types of pencils include mechanical pencils, which don't need sharpening; carpenters' pencils that have a flat, rectangular lead that makes broad, grainy marks as well as thin lines; and graphite sticks, which are extremely smooth, soft, and expressive in use.

CHARCOAL has a unique depth and richness for tonal studies. There are two types: willow and compressed. Willow is the most versatile. Compressed charcoal is darker and waxier and is more difficult to manipulate on the paper. There are also charcoal pencils, which are cleaner to handle and easier to control.

CONTE is made from compressed chalk and is available in stick and pencil form. It is one of the most attractive of all the monochrome materials, available in earth reds and browns, black, gray, and white. It has a pleasant tonal quality and color and is sensitive to the paper's texture.

PEN AND INK traditional dip pens, quills, reeds, and bamboos are light, flexible, and responsive and produce lively, animated marks. Rollerball and felt-tip pens and technical pens make more uniform lines, but you can break the line to achieve textural effects.

Drawing inks come in black and a range of colors.

COLOR MATERIALS

The wide range of color media that is available can be used in exciting and expressive ways.

CHALK PASTELS have a pleasing chalky, smudgy quality and come in a vast range of colors and tints. They can be used as either a drawing or painting medium, producing both sharp lines and powdery masses.

PASTEL PENCILS combine the "blendability" of chalk pastel with the convenience and versatility of pencil and are ideal for location sketching.

OIL PASTELS offer intense, vibrant colors and make thick, buttery strokes. Use them for bold, uninhibited statements of pure color.

COLORED PENCILS come in a wide range of hues and provide a portable tool for quick color notes. Though the colors cannot be blended, they can be overlaid to create lively optical mixes.

WATER-SOLUBLE PENCILS enable you to combine drawing and painting: you can spread the pigment with a brush into gentle washes of color.

WATERCOLOR

PASTEL PENCIL

OIL PASTEL

PAINT

WATER-SOLUBLE PENCIL

COLORED PENCIL

FELT-TIP

CHALK PASTEL

FELT-TIP pens may lack subtlety but they are extremely useful for capturing colorful atmospheres and encouraging a lively sketching style. They come in thin and broad-tipped varieties and in a large range of colors.

PAINTS, such as watercolor, gouache, and acrylic, are excellent for recording quick color impressions and can be combined with "dry" linear media to create complex effects of color and texture. They are also convenient, because you only need water to dilute them. Two or three colors are enough for sketching. A good-quality brush will hold plenty of paint for broad washes and also can come to a fine point for lines and details. Choose a reasonably-sized one — small brushes encourage tight, fiddly work.

CHOOSING A SKETCHBOOK

Sketchbooks come in a wide range of sizes and types. It is best to have two: a small one that fits easily into a pocket or bag for making on-the-spot sketches, and a larger one for making more considered drawings. Hardback sketchbooks are durable and allow you to work across a double-page spread if you want to. Spiral-bound pads allow you to remove pages without ruining the book. Type and quality of paper varies. Most are made with cartridge or bond paper. Also available are pads of tinted papers, ideal for pastel and conté work. Watercolor pads are made with quality watercolor paper and have a strong backing board for rigidity.

DRAWING ACCESSORIES

Try not to use erasers too much — a drawing should show its history in its marks. Plastic or kneaded putty erasers are best because they don't smudge. Drawings executed in pastel, charcoal, or very soft pencil should be sprayed with fixative to prevent smudging. If you draw on sheets of loose paper you will need a drawing board. Use masking tape or large clips to hold the paper in place.

A portable sketchbook is a must for on-the-spot sketches.

CHOOSING PAPERS

Some papers are more suitable for use with particular media than others. All papers have different surfaces, from smooth to highly textured. Pen and ink are best on smooth papers. Crumbly materials such as charcoal and pastel need a paper with enough surface "tooth" to hold the color. If you are using heavy washes of paint, use a thick paper that won't bend or cockle.

CARTRIDGE PAPER is a good all-purpose drawing paper for all media, particularly for pencil because it has a smooth surface.

BOND PAPER is smooth and creamy white in color, a good choice for pencil or pen work.

TINTED PAPERS A huge selection of colored papers is available, in bright and muted tones. Popular types include Ingres and Mi-Teintes. These papers are good for pastel, conté, and colored pencil work. The color of the paper plays a positive role in the drawing, complementing the subject.

WATERCOLOR PAPER can be used for drawing as well as painting. Smooth (hot-pressed) paper is good for pencil and ink. "Not" or cold-pressed paper has a textured surface that breaks up the strokes applied and gives a lively effect.

GETTING STARTED

If you want to draw, you don't have to wait for inspiration. Everywhere your eye falls, possible sketching subjects come to light. As Picasso declared, "I don't seek, I find." The simplest subject can make an inspired drawing: an old pair of shoes; a favorite armchair; a chance arrangement of things on the breakfast table. What is important is that you have something significant to say about it. Start by tackling simple subjects from around your home, drawing with pencil. Then move on to sketching your family and pets. Encouraged by success, you will gradually develop the confidence to tackle outdoor subjects.

INSPIRATION

If something inspires you, sketch it there and then — even if all you have at hand is the back of an envelope!

✳ TACKLE a variety of subjects to see which interests you most. Try different media and approaches, exploring aspects such as light and shade, color, or contour.

COMPOSITION

It is not always essential to create a formal composition when making a sketch, but if you are recording a subject as a basis for a painting it is important that the shapes, tones, and colors are organized in a balanced, harmonious way. In general, dividing the picture area into unequal sections is a reliable way to establish a pleasing composition.

VIEWFINDER

A viewfinder isolates the view, enabling you to select what to draw. Make one from two L-shaped pieces of black cardboard. Hold it up at arm's length, close one eye, and move your arm back and forth and side to side until the scene sits happily in the "window."

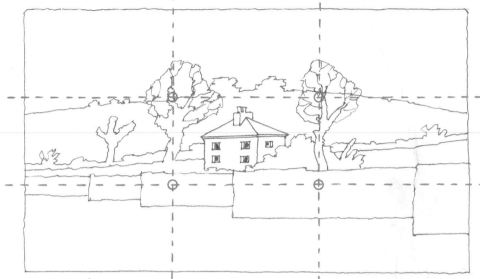

Mentally divide the paper into thirds both vertically and horizontally. Strong horizontal and vertical elements in the drawing can coincide with these lines. The points where the lines intersect are good places to locate the center of interest.

Make sure that the focus of interest is placed off-center and not in the middle of the drawing or at the edges. Look at the shapes made by different parts of the drawing and check that they balance each other.

Because the tree is a tall shape, an upright format is best. The sky area occupies one-third of the picture, the main subject two-thirds.

BASIC PERSPECTIVE

Linear perspective is a system used by artists to create a convincing illusion of three-dimensional form and space on a flat, two-dimensional piece of paper. When it's done successfully, the relative distance between objects, and their relative size, appear to the eye on paper just as they appear to the eye in real life. The basic principles of perspective are very straightforward.

✳ HORIZONTAL objects, like these chair arms, appear smaller and closer together the farther they are from the eye.

✳ FOREGROUND elements are bigger in relation to those farther back. People are halved in size as their distance from the viewer is doubled.

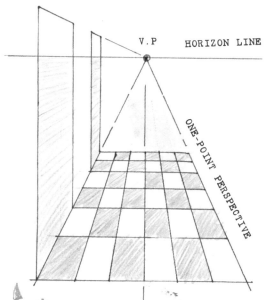

V.P   HORIZON LINE

ONE-POINT PERSPECTIVE

ALL YOU NEED TO KNOW

EYE LEVEL The height at which your eyes see an object.
HORIZON LINE Where the earth and sky seem to meet. This is always at eye level.
CONVERGING LINES Parallel lines appear to converge as they recede toward the horizon.
VANISHING POINT The point on the horizon where the converging lines meet.

✳ ONE-POINT perspective occurs when you look down a street or a corridor. All parallel lines — walls, fences, and so on — appear to converge on a single vanishing point on the horizon. All lines above eye level slant down toward the horizon line. All lines below eye level slant up toward the horizon line.

✳ TWO-POINT perspective occurs when two sides of an object, such as a building, are visible. Now there are two sets of parallel lines — one for each plane of the building — and each converges on its own vanishing point on the horizon.

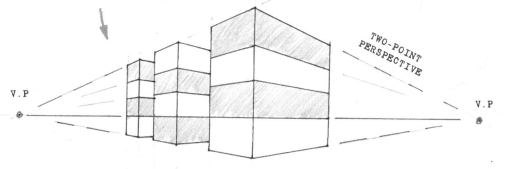

TWO-POINT PERSPECTIVE

V.P   V.P

19

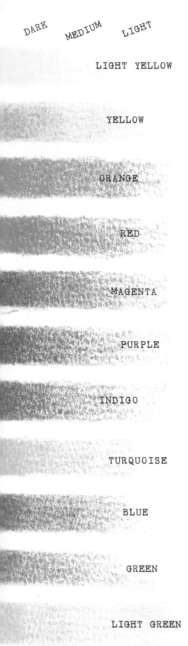

DARK   MEDIUM   LIGHT

LIGHT YELLOW

YELLOW

ORANGE

RED

MAGENTA

PURPLE

INDIGO

TURQUOISE

BLUE

GREEN

LIGHT GREEN

TONE AND COLOR

The word "tone" refers to how light or dark an object is, whatever its color. Every color has a tonal "value," ranging from white to black and with infinite shades of gray in between. You can see this by looking at the two drawings opposite, one in color and the other in monochrome. It is important to be able to see colors in terms of tone so that you can create a unified and interesting composition by balancing the tonal "weight" of one color against that of another.

* DIFFERENT colors similar tones

* TONAL scale from dark to light. Tonal gradations were achieved by varying the line density.

Experiment with tone and color using different colored pencils, pastels, and inks.

"White Cup and Saucer" (1864)
IGNACE HENRI JEAN FANTIN-LATOUR
(1836-1904).

"Still Life"
SAMUEL JOHN
PEPLOE
(1871-1935).

SKETCHING EVERYDAY OBJECTS

Practice drawing by studying simple objects from around your home. There is hardly anything that isn't "drawable"; a couple of onions sitting on a table will give you plenty to explore in terms of color, form, texture, and line.

GETTING IT IN PERSPECTIVE

Knowing how to draw squares and circles in perspective is essential when drawing indoor objects such as bottles, cups, chairs, and tables. The same principles can be applied to outdoor subjects such as buildings.

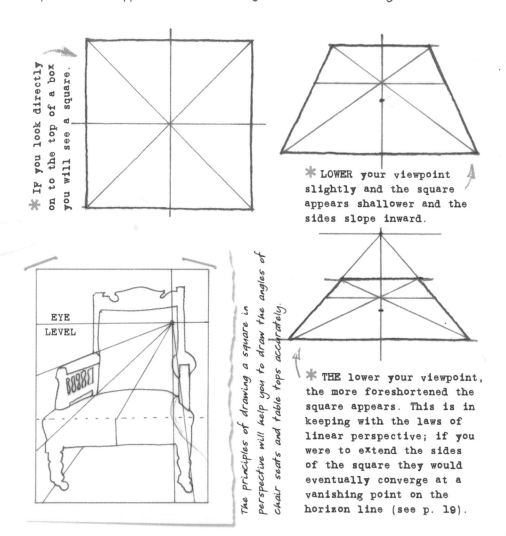

* If you look directly on to the top of a box you will see a square.

* LOWER your viewpoint slightly and the square appears shallower and the sides slope inward.

EYE LEVEL

The principles of drawing a square in perspective will help you to draw the angles of chair seats and table tops accurately.

* THE lower your viewpoint, the more foreshortened the square appears. This is in keeping with the laws of linear perspective; if you were to extend the sides of the square they would eventually converge at a vanishing point on the horizon line (see p. 19).

SQUARING THE CIRCLE

Just as you see less and less of the top of the box the lower your eye level is, so you will see less and less of the opening of a cup or a bowl. The circular shape flattens out and becomes an ellipse shape. The lower your viewpoint, the shallower the ellipse will be.

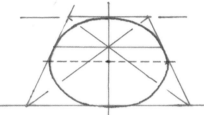

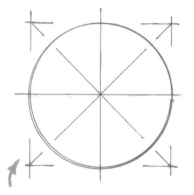

✳ THINK of the circle as fitting into a square. The center of the circle is at the intersection of the square's diagonals.

✳ IF you draw that square in perspective, you can then draw a perfect ellipse to fit inside it. Note that the center of the ellipse is not at the intersection of the square's diagonals—it is halfway between the front and back lines of the square (shown by the dotted line).

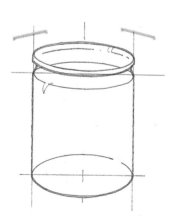

Look at a glass jar and note how the ellipse at the top, which is nearer, is flatter than that at the base, which is farther away.

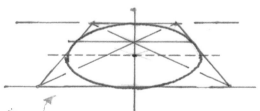

✳ DRAW the curves of the ellipse so that they touch the center points of the square, passing through the diagonals.

MODELING FORM

We are able to "read" three-dimensional objects because of the light that falls on them. Without light, and the shadows it creates, all objects would appear as flat shapes. The diagrams on the opposite page show how patterns of light and shade are formed on solid objects. Each shape has a definite light side and shadow side. Notice the sharp division between light and shadow where one plane meets another on the cube and the pyramid; compare this with the gradual transition from light to shadow on the sphere and cylinder.

Charcoal is ideal for making tonal drawings.

Put in the shadow areas with gentle hatching and shading, gradually increasing the pressure of shading in the areas that you want to be darker.

All the forms in nature are combinations of simple geometric shapes —
spheres, cylinders, cubes, cones, and pyramids. A tree is basically a
sphere on top of a cylinder, mountains are variations of the cone and
the pyramid, and so on. These shapes can be used to clarify your
understanding of any object, and how light
and shadow define its form.

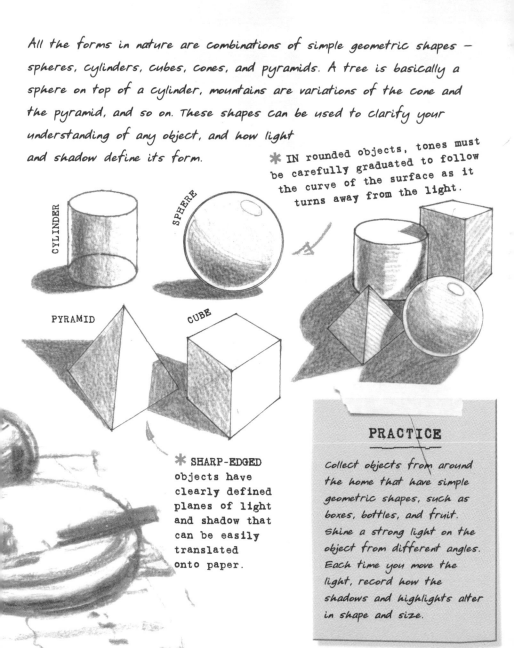

✷ IN rounded objects, tones must
be carefully graduated to follow
the curve of the surface as it
turns away from the light.

CYLINDER

SPHERE

PYRAMID

CUBE

✷ SHARP-EDGED
objects have
clearly defined
planes of light
and shadow that
can be easily
translated
onto paper.

PRACTICE

Collect objects from around
the home that have simple
geometric shapes, such as
boxes, bottles, and fruit.
Shine a strong light on the
object from different angles.
Each time you move the
light, record how the
shadows and highlights alter
in shape and size.

DRAWING WITH PENCIL

Pencil is the most immediate and enjoyable of all drawing media to use. It can be broad and painterly like charcoal or incisive like a pen. The quality and nuance of a pencil line is influenced by the grade of pencil used, pressure applied, speed of the line, and texture of the paper. Pencils glide over smooth paper and give clean, unbroken lines; on rough paper the bumps "catch" the pencil mark, producing soft, grainy lines and tones.

✳ SOFT pencils wear down quickly. Sharpen a pencil with a blade to create a long tapering cone that can be used on its side for drawing broadly. Pencil sharpeners eat up too much wood before coming to a point, and give too short a point.

PRACTICE

To discover the wide range of effects possible with a simple pencil, try out hard and soft grades on different types of paper. Practice making light and dark tones by varying the pressure on the pencil or by varying the space between hatched and crosshatched strokes.

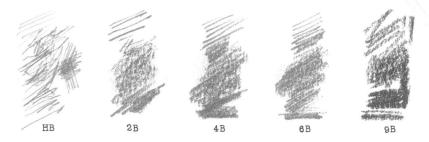

| HB | 2B | 4B | 6B | 9B |

DIFFERENT GRADES OF PENCIL *Pencils are graded according to the hardness or softness of the lead. There is normally a choice of 12 grades, from very hard (9H) to very soft (9B). Grade HB is midway between the two. Hard pencils make fine, silvery lines, while soft pencils give more varied lines and can be used on their sides to produce solid areas of tone.*

DRAWING WITH CHARCOAL

The soft, grainy quality of charcoal makes it a uniquely expressive medium, capable of producing rich, velvety blacks and soft, misty grays. The tip of the stick will produce strong and vigorous lines, while the side can be used to lay down broad marks. Rich tonal effects can be achieved by blending and smudging with your fingertip or with a paper stump, and highlights can be picked out with a putty eraser. Charcoal is an excellent medium for beginners because it forces you to draw broadly and not get lost in detail. It is also a forgiving medium, easy to correct by rubbing marks off with a finger or a tissue.

TIP

When sketching with charcoal, choose a textured paper rather than a smooth one. The grain of the paper picks up and holds more charcoal, making it easier to produce rich, dark tones. When you finish a drawing, always spray it with fixative to prevent any accidental smudging.

✳ BLENDING
Rub with a short
piece of charcoal
on its side to
make solid darks.

✳ CROSS-HATCHING
Build up tones in
a sketch with
hatched and cross-
hatched lines.

✳ SMUDGING
Use your fingertip
to blend and
lighten tones.

DRAWING WITH INK

Drawing with pen and ink may seem a daunting prospect because you can't rub out mistakes. But it is this very restriction that makes ink so exciting to use. It forces you to concentrate, to make every line count, and your drawing and observational skills will quickly improve as a result. Ink is a highly expressive and sympathetic medium. A simple pen outline can capture the essence of a subject.

Using very fine lines enables you to produce a drawing full of detail and subtle tones.

A rich and variable range of tones and textures can be obtained using fine hatching and crosshatching. You can also combine line drawing with washes of color or tone, using either ink or watercolor applied with a brush.

SOLID

PRACTICE

Experiment with different pens and the marks they make. Traditional dip pens, reed pens, and quill pens are flexible and make expressive, fluctuating lines. Modern fountain pens, ballpoints, and technical pens give a continuous, unvarying line for a graphic effect.

LINE AND WASH

CROSS-HATCHING

SCRIBBLE

A wide range of tonal effects can be obtained with India ink using a pen or a brush.

"Dutch
Interior"
PIETER
JANSSENS
(1623-82).

"The Bedroom" (1909) CARL LARSSON
(1853-1919).

"Vincent's Chair" (1888) VINCENT VAN GOGH (1853-90).

SKETCHING INDOORS

Domestic interiors, part of everyday life, can be a rich source of material for your sketches. Themes include incidental "still lifes," such as a pitcher of flowers on a windowsill or the clutter of the breakfast table; interesting effects of light, color, and perspective; the surface textures and patterns of the objects in the room; and views glimpsed through an open door or window.

SHAPES AND SPACES

When you draw an interior scene, you not only have to get the perspective of the room right, you also have to draw the objects within it in perspective and to the correct scale. If you train your eye to see accurately you will soon become accustomed to judging proportion and scale and the relation of one thing to another in a composition. There are devices that will help you to check the accuracy of your drawing and these can be useful, but try to rely on your own observation and use these methods only as a means of double checking.

Use your pencil as an aid to proportions and spatial relationships. Hold the pencil at arm's length. Line it up against the subject, close one eye, and move your thumbnail along the pencil to take the required measurement. Use this key measurement as a yardstick against which to measure and compare other dimensions in the subject.

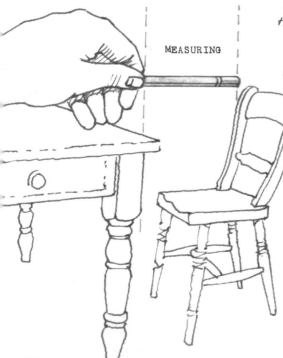

MEASURING

PRACTICE

Try drawing all the negative shapes around a simple subject, rather than the subject itself. With careful observation, you should achieve a fairly accurate positive shape of the subject "trapped" by its surrounding negative spaces.

POSITIVE AND NEGATIVE SHAPES

A picture has positive shapes (the objects) and negative shapes (the spaces between the objects). Negative shapes are just as important as positive ones, contributing to the overall design. These negatives also enable you to check the accuracy of your drawing. When you draw chairs and tables, for example, look at the shapes between the legs and crossbars; if these "negatives" look right, the chances are that the positives are accurate.

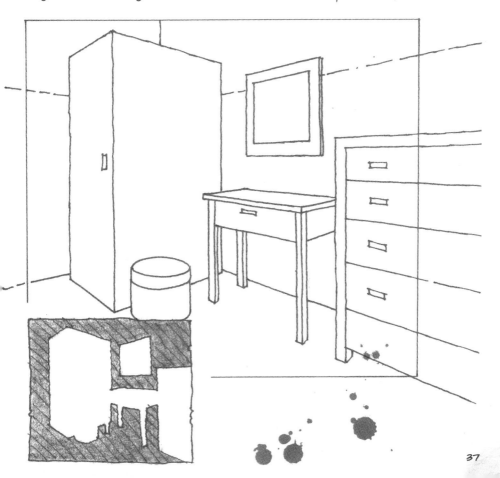

DIFFERENT INTERIORS

Making sketches of the rooms in your own home will develop your skills and give you the confidence to tackle interiors in public buildings. You will find a wealth of sketching subjects in cafés, bars, and restaurants; shops and indoor markets; galleries and museums; concert halls and theaters; railway stations and airport lounges; factories, workshops, and offices.

Remember you don't have to record every last detail; the important thing is to capture the atmosphere and observe the interaction of figures and their surroundings.

TIP

Use a fast medium such as a 6B pencil; this lends itself to quick action studies and gives a full tonal range. Alternatively, use a reservoir pen, which forces you to make clear decisions instantly. For tonal variations you can moisten a finger and smudge the areas where you want to bring out a form.

* CAFÉS and bars have always been a favorite subject for artists because they combine elements of still life (table settings and food), figure drawing (diners and waiters), and architecture (the interior itself). Use a small sketchbook and a simple pencil or pen so you can sketch unnoticed.

PRACTICE

In the enclosed environment of a room, the light is channeled through the relatively small area of a window, creating interesting patterns of light and shadow in the room itself and on the objects within it. Make a monochrome sketch of a favorite room, thinking about the balance of lights and darks.

"Van Gogh's Bedroom" VINCENT VAN GOGH (1853-90).

PERSPECTIVE Drawing an interior is challenging: not only do you have to get the perspective of the room right because any errors will be immediately obvious, you also have to draw the objects within the room in perspective and to the correct scale. Perspective in interiors works in exactly the same way as it does out of doors (see pages 18-19): the parallel tops and bottoms of walls doors and windows recede toward the same vanishing point on the horizon line of floorboards.

Try sketching or xeroxing an interior scene and drawing in the perspective lines of the walls, floors, and furniture.

Start by drawing the vertical and horizontal lines of the far wall. Then establish the position of the horizon line by holding your pencil at arm's length, horizontally, at eye level. Draw the receding lines of the side walls. They should meet at your center of vision on the horizon line.

※ WHEN drawing a chair, draw lines around it to form a cube. Its parallel lines converge at an imaginary vanishing point behind the chair.

43

INSIDE
LOOKING OUT

An interior scene takes
on a whole new dimension
when you include the
additional space that can
be seen through a window
or an open door. Depicting
a part of the inside of
the room as well as what
can be glimpsed outside
it creates an intriguing
double image — a frame
within a frame.

PRACTICE

Position yourself near a
window or doorway that
frames an interesting view
and draw what you see. Try
to convey the contrast
between the bright outdoor
light and the relatively
dark, cool interior light.

Study the interior scenes of masters such as Vermeer,
Van Gogh, Matisse, and Bonnard for inspiration.

A fully or partially open door that gives a tantalizing glimpse of the room beyond excites our curiosity, and the framework of horizontals and verticals makes an intriguing composition.

45

"Two Cats" FRANZ MARC (1880-1916).

"Busy Bodies and Busy Bees" LUCY ANN LEAVERS (1845-1915).

SKETCHING ANIMALS

Sketching animals is both a delight and a challenge, for they don't keep still for long. Start close to home, by sketching your own pet. If you develop an interest in this subject you can go on to draw the animals on farms, in zoos, and in the wild, exploring different ways of conveying movement, character, and the texture and markings of fur and feathers.

ANIMAL ANATOMY

You've got to build a house before you can decorate it, and similarly you must draw a solid animal before you consider the markings on its surface. You don't need a textbook knowledge of anatomy in order to sketch your pet, but an

awareness that beneath all that fur there is a body and skeleton will give your sketches more conviction. Start by looking at the general proportions of your subject: the shape and tilt of the head and its size in relation to the body, the angle and length of the legs, and the overall posture.

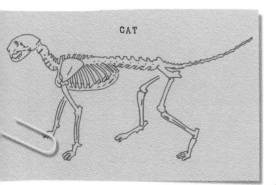

CAT

* CATS have about 230 bones, held together by more than 500 muscles. No wonder they can get into so many strange positions!

DOG

* IN order to
understand the
form of an
animal and the
way it moves,
it helps to be
aware of the
underlying
skeleton even
when it cannot
be seen.

Even though the body is covered with
fur, you can learn a lot about the
underlying anatomy of your pet cat,
dog, or rabbit by handling and stroking
it and watching how it moves.

FUR AND FEATHERS

When you're drawing animals, you'll find that their patterns and markings help to describe the underlying form. Bear in mind, however, that too much attention to surface detail can make the animal look stiff and lifeless. Don't try to draw every spot, stripe, hair, or feather. Observe where the most distinctive markings are and use them to emphasize the shape of the animal in key places such as around the head and shoulders and the rump.

Tabby stripes follow the contours of the body and thus describe the cat's form.

The intricate structure of a feather is one of nature's marvels.

* THE colors and
textures of fur,
feathers, skin, and
scales are a rewarding
area for individual
sketchbook studies.
Try to find marks
that will represent
them with conviction.

SKETCHING CATS

The supreme grace and beauty of the feline form have fascinated artists for thousands of years. Start by sketching your cat sleeping. This gives you a chance to learn about structure and proportions, which will enable you to draw a moving cat quickly and accurately. Then sketch him when he is grooming. The cat will stay in the same place but perform a series of repeated movements, which will allow you to record the rhythmic grace of the pose.

*CATS are capable of great speed and agility, and also of absolute stillness. Mostly the latter.

Ink and wash convey line, texture, and form.

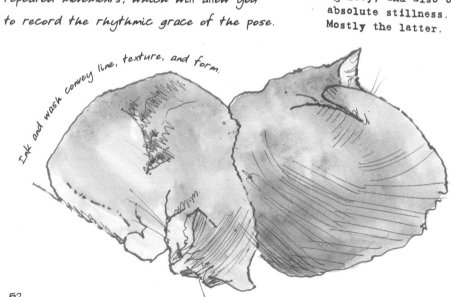

A ballpoint pen makes fluid lines that skate nimbly around the sinuous feline form.

Light and shadow describe form.

* AS you draw, make rhythmic gestures with your pen or pencil. Use fluid strokes that correspond to the sinuous contours of the cat.

A cat's head fits into a rough hexagonal shape from almost any angle. Notice that the base of the ear starts on the forehead, not on the top of the head. The fur grows outward away from the eyes and mouth, indicating the structure of the face.

53

SKETCHING DOGS
Unlike a cat, a well-trained dog might be persuaded to "sit!" while you sketch. Don't attempt to draw every hair and whisker but try to convey what's special about your dog. He may have floppy ears, a soppy smile, or a "hangdog" expression, and endearing qualities like these make a portrait sketch come alive.

PRACTICE
Photos are a great starting point for an animal drawing. It is best not to copy them directly because they freeze the action and flatten details, but they are a useful way of studying the relationship of nose to eyes and ears, and the angle of the head to the body, and so on.

Photos are useful for studying structure and proportions – whatever the pose!

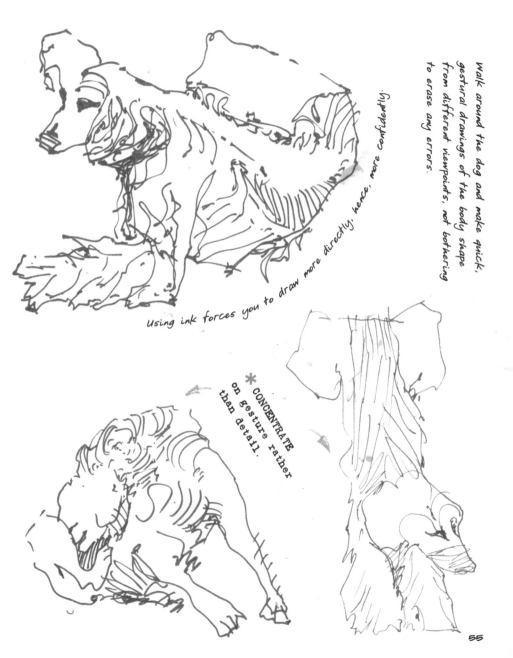

Walk around the dog and make quick, gestural drawings of the body shape from different viewpoints, not bothering to erase any errors.

Using ink forces you to draw more directly; hence, more confidently.

* CONCENTRATE on gesture rather than detail.

Draw with broken lines that give a sense of movement.

Don't stop to correct mistakes. Keep the lines moving, keep the sketch moving.

Don't worry if one bird flies off when you are in mid-sketch; another will probably adopt the same pose, allowing you to finish it.

56

BIRDS IN FLIGHT

Patient observation is the key to success when sketching birds in flight. Study their silhouettes against the sky and limit yourself to a few quick, gestural strokes with the pencil. Use a large sketchbook and cover several pages with studies of birds on the ground and in flight. Identify and simplify the characteristic shape of the species, its stance, the tilt of its head.

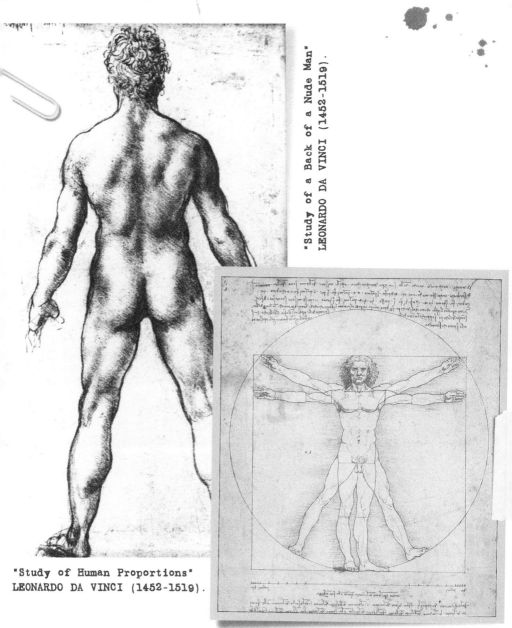

"Study of a Back of a Nude Man"
LEONARDO DA VINCI (1452-1519).

"Study of Human Proportions"
LEONARDO DA VINCI (1452-1519).

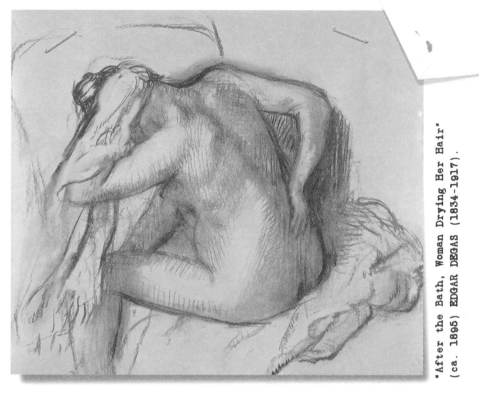

SKETCHING PEOPLE

It is often said that if you can draw the human figure you will be able to draw just about anything. Skill in drawing figures comes from observation, an understanding of anatomy and proportion, and above all, practice. And there is no better place to practice your skills than in your sketchbook.

INSIDE OUT A knowledge of human anatomy is not essential to figure drawing, but it certainly helps. Familiarity with the bones and muscles that lie beneath the skin will help you to understand the proportions of the body, its structure, and the way that it moves. You will be able to draw figures with much greater conviction if you know exactly what each bump and curve actually means.

As you draw, make lines that swell and taper to express the active and passive contours of the body.

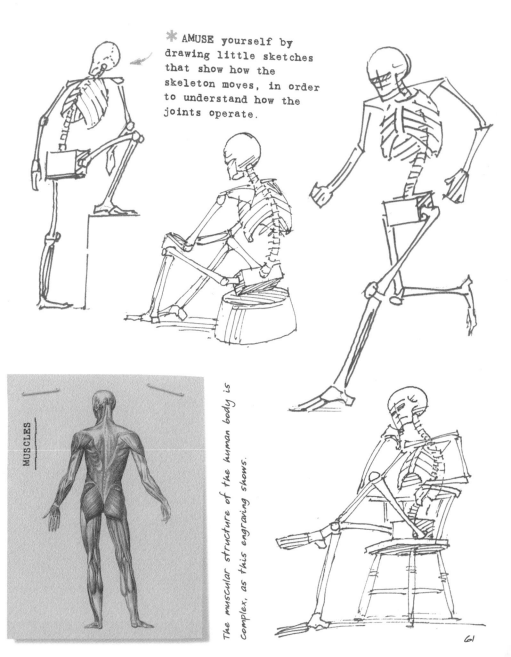

* AMUSE yourself by drawing little sketches that show how the skeleton moves, in order to understand how the joints operate.

MUSCLES

The muscular structure of the human body is complex, as this engraving shows.

61

MEASURING AND PROPORTION

Although no two people are exactly alike, it is useful to know the proportions of the 'ideal' figure and keep these in mind as you draw. According to classical proportions, the average adult body is between seven and eight heads tall. This is a useful guide, but is no substitute for direct observation. People's legs can be short or long in proportion to their bodies, for example, and it is important to record these characteristics.

The elbow is about halfway down the arm.

The legs start about halfway down the body.

* THE knee is about halfway down the leg.

MEASURING

Hold a pencil at arm's length and use it to compare the angle or dimension of one part of the figure against another. Line up your pencil against the subject, close one eye, and move your thumbnail up or down to take the required measurement.

✳ **WHEN** the weight is on one leg, the angle of the shoulders runs contrary to the angle of the hips so that the body balances.

The human body is symmetrical, so when even a small movement is made on one side, the other side has to compensate in order to stay upright. For example, when one side of the body stretches, the other contracts. To determine the main directional lines of a figure's pose, start by lightly marking out the horizontal axes of the shoulders, hips, and knees.

Line and wash effectively describes the contours and modeling of the figure and conveys a lively sense of movement.

Subtle variations in light and shade can be obtained with varying densities of hatching and crosshatching. The strokes can either follow or cross the forms.

FORM AND VOLUME

To convey the form and
solidity of the human body,
you have to think in terms of
mass and volume as well as line.
It is a mistake to draw a solid
outline and then shade it in; the figure will look flat and wooden.
Start with light, feathery strokes and then apply more pressure along the
"active" contours such as the curve of the hips, calves, and buttocks.
Work over the whole figure at once, putting down the broad masses of
tone at the same time as you draw the contours.

SKETCHING HEADS

Few subjects offer more challenge to an artist than the human head; nothing else has quite the same combination of compulsive interest and infinite variety.

Although it is important to recognize that no two heads are exactly alike, and that only by observing a person carefully can you hope to produce a good likeness, it is essential to have a grasp of the physical structure of the head. A knowledge of the proportions of the face will enable you to produce accurate and sensitive sketches.

An infant has a much bigger cranium relative to the face than an adult.

Viewed from the side and front, notice how large the cranial part of the skull is in comparison with the "mask" area (the eyes, the nose, and the mouth). Try to think of this basic skull shape underlying the face and describe it as you draw.

✳ THINK like a cartoonist. Try to convey character with just a few lines, concentrating on the essential features.

✳ WHEN the head is tilted at an angle, the features appear compressed.

EGG-HEADS From the front the head is shaped like an egg, with the pointed end down. Draw the outline of the head, then draw a line down the center to mark the position of the nose and mouth. Draw a line across the center to mark the position of the eyes. Draw a line halfway below that to mark the tip of the nose. Repeat to find the position of the lower lip. The ears line up between the eyebrows and the tip of the nose. The hairline is about one-third down from the top.

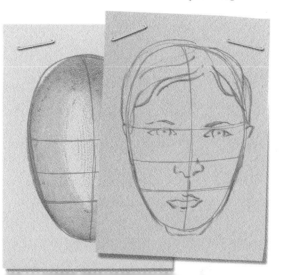

SKETCHING HANDS AND FEET

The hands are one of the most expressive parts of the body, but their complex shapes can be tricky to draw. In the 18th century, artists would charge more for a portrait with two hands rather than one! Three main shapes make up the hand: the thumb, fingers, and palm. Start by drawing these sections as simple blocks and rectangles. Then refine the contours; look at how each finger relates to the next, and the shapes between them. Then model the planes of light and shadow with hatching, making the strokes follow the direction of the bone structure and muscles.

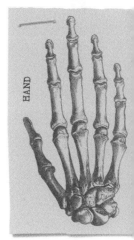

HAND

The width across the knuckles is about the same as the length of the fingers.

The fingers are about half the length of the hand.

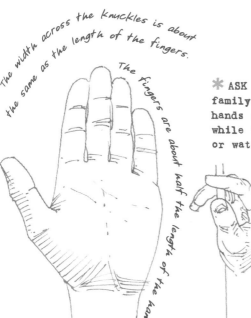

✳ ASK your friends or family to keep their hands still for you while they are reading or watching television.

The feet, too, are vital parts of life drawing, particularly in a standing pose, because they take all the weight of the figure. As with the hands, treat the feet as overall shapes before observing them in more intricate detail. The hands and feet are surprisingly large; from base to tip they are almost as long as the face and about half as wide.

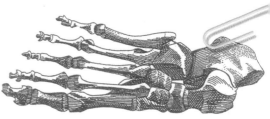

FOOT

The bones in the foot are surprisingly long, given how small our toes appear!

✳ MAKE sketches of a friend's feet. Fill a whole sketchbook page with them, viewed from every conceivable angle. Note that the feet are set obliquely to the leg rather than pointing directly forward.

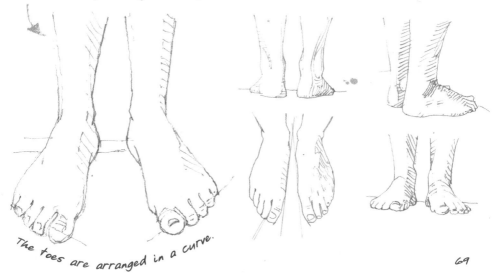

The toes are arranged in a curve.

SKETCHING FAMILY AND FRIENDS

If you feel inhibited about sketching people in public places, remember that your family and friends are just as interesting to draw as anyone else! You don't even have to ask them to pose — just capture them at quiet moments such as when they are reading or watching television. When your subject is relaxed you will find it

The interaction between individuals and groups of people can make some interesting compositions.

easier to capture his or her personality and expression. Household activities such as ironing, gardening, or cooking are interesting to draw and will give you practice in sketching moving figures.

✳ TAKE the opportunity to "tell a story" with your sketch by emphasizing the character traits of your subject and by adding suggestions of background.

PRACTICE

Carry a small sketchbook
with you at all times and
make quick sketches of
faces you see around you.
Emphasize the features
that best express the
individual and even slightly
exaggerate them; the element
of caricature is contained
in all good likenesses.

CATCHING A LIKENESS

In trying to capture a likeness, don't launch too soon on those tempting details of the features. Think first about the shape of the head and its tilt, the set of the jaw, and the general demeanor of the person. Look for the dominant angles, masses, and shapes before you start to put in details. The proportions of the face are unique to each individual. Use your pencil as a measuring tool to check one feature in relation to another and gauge angles and distances. Where does the corner of the eye lie in relation to the corner of the mouth? How does the width of the head compare to the length?

✻ PRACTICE sketching a portrait using pencil to begin with; you can then graduate to ink when you feel more confident about capturing the finer details.

LIFE DRAWING

The best way to practice drawing the nude figure is to join a life class, where you can study professional models under the guidance of a tutor. Life drawing teaches a thorough understanding of the forms and proportions of the body and develops skill at representing movement and gesture.

PRACTICE

Make a series of five-minute sketches of the figure using a fast medium such as charcoal or conté. This forces you to eliminate fussy details and get the gesture down fast. It's an excellent "warm-up exercise" that frees up your drawing hand before you tackle a more measured, disciplined drawing of the figure.

Use variations of line weight and tone to express the rhythms and tensions of the body.

Try to understand the pose before you start to work. Draw lightly at first, moving with your arm, not your fingers, swiftly sketching out the complete figure. Only when you have something resembling the pose should you return to specific areas and tighten them up.

* PROPS such as chairs, cushions, and drapes are useful for putting the figure into context and making the model more comfortable!

"Lucie Leon at the
Piano" (ca. 1892)
BERTHE MORISOT
(1841-1895).

"Mother and Child" (1897) MARY CASSATT (1844-1926).

SKETCHING CHILDREN Children
have a universal appeal and are less self-
conscious and more spontaneous and natural
than adults. They make a particularly rewarding
subject to draw, especially for the sketcher
who also happens to be a doting parent!

YOUNG CHILDREN

Lively and inquisitive, young children quickly become bored if asked to pose for a drawing. It is much better to sketch children when they are absorbed in reading, watching television, or playing. This way, the child remains reasonably still but the gestures and expressions are mobile and lifelike. Make several sketches on a single sheet and think less about achieving a likeness than defining the main shapes of the body and the characteristic movements of the activity.

* CHILDREN are at their most natural when engaged in a favorite activity. Their obvious enjoyment and absorption can make fascinating study.

Develop your speed and confidence by making quick gestural drawings.

As the child develops, the face lengthens, and the contours of the nose, mouth, and jaw are more pronounced. The eyes are still large but appear smaller in relation to the face than those of a young child.

79

DRAWING BABIES

If there is a baby or young toddler in the house, it is a good idea to keep your sketching materials close at hand so that you can sketch whenever an opportunity occurs. Babies are surprisingly difficult to draw because their forms and features are soft and formless compared to those of an adult. Prolonged preliminary observation is the key to success. A young baby has a very large head in comparison to the rest of the body, with very large, round cheeks and hardly any visible neck. Note also the tiny size of the nose, the mouth, and the ears in relation to the head.

Practice drawing sleeping babies before you tackle wriggling ones! Use a very sharp H-grade pencil to suggest the fine hairs and smooth features. Avoid hard outlines and too much detail; leave plenty of paper untouched to describe the smoothness and roundness of the face.

"Children of Charles I"
SIR ANTHONY VAN DYCK (1599-1641).

* IN babies and toddlers, the cranium and forehead are proportionately larger than those of an adult and the facial features appear to be set much closer together. The nose, the mouth, and the chin are tiny and soft, and the eyes are large and round.

OLDER CHILDREN

As children grow older they are fascinating and challenging subjects to draw because they combine the charm and innocence of childhood with the self-consciousness of approaching adolescence. Older children may be more willing to pose for you now, but they will probably affect an expression of bored indifference while doing so!

Clothing is an important means of self-expression for a young person.

PROPORTIONS

Bodily proportions change
radically as a child grows
up. In babies, the body
measures roughly four heads
tall and the legs are short.
A child's body measures
between five and six heads
tall, depending on its age.
This is only a rough guide
since children grow at
different rates, so use your
pencil as a measuring tool to
check that the proportions
of your sitter are correct.

✳ YOU may find that
a bold medium such as
charcoal or felt-tip
pen best expresses the
lean, angular shapes
and slightly awkward
gestures and attitudes
of a young person.

"The Skirts of a
Wood" (1825)
SAMUEL PALMER
(1805-81).

"Sea and Clouds" SIR WILLIAM
BLAKE RICHMOND (1842-1921).

SKETCHING
LANDSCAPE

For many people the term landscape conjures up an image of a broad vista or a picturesque view, but this is not the only way of interpreting the theme. It can just as easily be a study of a gnarled tree trunk or a corner of your own garden. Add to this the myriad effects of light and weather that can transform a scene, and you have enough subjects to keep you sketching for a lifetime.

UP THE GARDEN PATH

If you are fortunate enough to have a garden, you have your own private "landscape" right on your doorstep. It will provide you with sketching material throughout the seasons, from studies of individual plants and flowers to "still lifes" of plant pots and watering cans, to detailed compositions featuring trees, buildings, and figures. Sketching in a garden avoids the curious onlooker, and will help to build up your confidence before venturing farther afield. Walk around your garden, viewfinder in hand: suddenly the boringly familiar will present new and exciting possibilities!

*USE a soft medium such as pastel or watercolor to capture the essential gestures of plants and flowers.

Explore ways of creating texture using line alone. Use a pen or sharp pencil to suggest flowers, foliage, and grass with loose scribbles, tight crosshatching, and quick flecks.

OUTDOOR SKETCHING

Working outdoors can be difficult because you have to cope with changing light and weather conditions, marauding insects, and curious passersby. But when you can feel the warmth of the sun, hear the birds chirping, and smell the sweet grass, all of your senses are alive and this will show in the vitality of your sketches. Don't waste time looking for the "ideal" view. Trust your instincts — when something catches your eye, sketch your first impression there and then. Keep your field kit simple and practical. A hardback sketchbook does away with the need for something to lean on, and bulldog clips or rubber bands will keep the pages down in windy conditions. A retractable pencil means you don't need a sharpener.

✳ IF you want to emphasize an interesting
sky, position the horizon low in the drawing.
If you want to emphasize features of the
landscape, place the horizon high.

Watercolor is ideal for capturing the
fleeting effects of light and weather on
the landscape. Just two or three colors
will give a wide range of subtle tones.

PLANNING A COMPOSITION

It is helpful to isolate a part of the landscape by looking through a viewfinder made from two L-shaped pieces of cardboard. Restricting your view of the landscape stops your eye from taking in too much and clarifies the composition. If several aspects of the scene interest you, make a series of thumbnail sketches. Look for the big shapes and tones. Simplify the scene by breaking it down into areas based on sky, horizon, and foreground.

Make rapid sketches to see
how the composition looks on
paper. You will be surprised at
the difference in emotional
effect that even a slight change
of viewpoint can produce.

Pencil is ideal for making thumbnail sketches because you can get down the features, the shapes of clouds, and the positions of shadows quickly.

Dramatic compositions are to be found
where the sea meets the beach.

WATERSCAPES

Water presents the sketcher with plenty of inspiration. Lakes, rivers, and streams provide a calm, rhythmic element in landscapes; with beaches and harbors, the vast expanses of sky and water are set against the land's edge and all the bustling activity it contains; and wet roads and sidewalks reflect the bright lights of the city. Water, like the sky, is constantly moving and changing. You have to look for the most significant waves, ripples, and reflections and quickly put them down on the paper. Pastels, pen and ink, and charcoal are well suited to this kind of rapid drawing.

* OVERLAPPING is a simple
method of explaining depth.
As soon as one thing is
placed in front of another,
like the hills in this
sketch, you create a feeling
of receding space.

AERIAL PERSPECTIVE

As objects become more distant, the intervening atmospheric haze softens edges and lessens contrasts. This effect is called aerial perspective and is the means by which you can conjure up, on a small piece of paper, a panorama of fields, hills, and trees stretching as far as the eye can see. Observe and record how tone, color, and detail are strongest in the foreground and fade gradually toward the horizon, often disappearing into a misty haze where sky meets land.

SKIES AND CLOUDS
Follow in the footsteps of Constable and Turner and keep a sketchbook just for skies, making on-the-spot sketches of different cloud types and patterns. Cloud studies can be beautiful things in their own right and will provide you with invaluable reference material for your paintings. Skies can change rapidly, so use a broad medium. Delightful, rapid effects can be obtained with charcoal, chalk, and pastel, especially on tinted paper. They can be smudged for drifting, wispy clouds, or used strongly for storm clouds. The transparency of watercolor is ideally suited to painting soft clouds and misty skies.

The sky recedes just as the land does, so be aware of the effects of perspective in clouds. They gradually get smaller, flatter, and weaker as they get farther away, and some are partly obscured by others.

✳ **KEEP** your drawing simple. Look for the big shapes and principal tonal contrasts. Let the paper itself give a feeling of space and air.

PRACTICE

Animals (and figures) can lend life and animation, and a sense of scale, to your landscape drawings. This is where your sketchbook studies can come in useful: you can "borrow" sketches of individual animals and transpose them to a landscape scene that might otherwise look quite empty. Group the animals together attractively and have some overlapping, so that they move the eye through the landscape.

"Krumau on the Molde" (1912) EGON SCHIELE (1890-1918).

SKETCHING BUILDINGS

Streets and buildings are a readily accessible subject and offer an ideal opportunity to practice your skills in observation, mark-making, and perspective drawing. There are many aspects to explore in the urban environment, from closely observed details of individual buildings to bustling street scenes. The complex arrangements of walls and rooftops and the varied colors and textures of buildings invite interpretation in a way that is unique to you.

PERSPECTIVE

To render the solid, three-dimensional form of buildings, it helps if you can find a corner of a street so that two sides of the building are visible rather than one. The oblique lines of the street create a sense of depth and recession and lend added interest to the composition. A knowledge of perspective is useful when tackling street scenes, but not vital for the sketcher. An active line quality and some distortions can add greatly to the vitality of a sketch.

CONSTRUCTING BUILDINGS

All parallel lines will seem to converge toward a vanishing point or points on the horizon line. Often, one or both vanishing points will be off to either side of your paper, so you need to check the angles of rooftops etc.

103

Use bold lines and color blocks to capture the charm of old buildings.

104

ARCHITECTURAL DETAILS

When you are walking around a town or city, keep a sketchbook handy and draw any details that catch your eye. Remember to look up as you wander — there are many interesting features to be viewed above street level. Architectural details such as doorways, windows, arches, balconies, and decorative moldings can make fascinating subjects in themselves. When drawing buildings, try to relate the details to the underlying structure from the start rather than tagging them on at the end. It isn't necessary to draw every window, brick, and roof tile — a small area of texture can imply the whole. With experience, you will develop a kind of visual shorthand that suggests rather than laboriously copies the details of buildings.

Contrast detailed areas with sketchier passages so as not to overload the drawing.

✳ USE fine hatching with a pen or a hard pencil to convey intricate details.

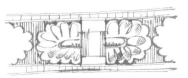

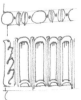

SKETCHING ON VACATION

Whenever you travel on vacation, use your sketchbook to record your interpretation of the unique character of that region. When you are in an unfamiliar location everything seems new and fascinating, and you look at your surroundings with a fresh eye. You don't have to record grand cathedrals and ancient monuments; away from the crowded tourist spots you will find secluded back streets that are full of architectural interest. Sketch anything that represents, for you, the atmosphere of the place — details of ornate old buildings, a colorful street market, a bustling fishing harbor, a hilltop village — and include people in your sketches to add life and animation.

You look at a subject intensely when you draw it, and you will find that your sketches evoke memories in a way that photos cannot.

✳ USE your sketchbook as
a visual diary of your
trip, filling a page with
a combination of images
evoking time and place.

ROOM WITH A VIEW

You don't even have to leave your hotel room in order to capture the atmosphere of a foreign place. The view from an upstairs window or balcony offers a different perspective that reveals surprising details. The complex, layered patterns of rooftops, for instance, form an intriguing geometry of angular lines and shapes. And you can sketch without being overlooked by strangers!

✳ INCLUDE details of interiors, too. Details such as furniture, window shutters, and balconies give a flavor of the locale.

Drawing with a felt-tip pen forces
you to concentrate on the essentials
that capture the character of a place.

"In the Rain" (1882) VINCENT VAN GOGH (1853-90).

"The Round" (ca. 1884) CAMILLE PISSARO (1831-1903).

PEOPLE AND PLACES

Sketching on-the-spot in public places forces
you to work with speed and develop rapid
methods of notation. You will find that it
injects a fresh vitality and confidence
into your sketches, and your sketchbook
becomes a fascinating visual diary of people,
places, and events you have seen.

TRAVEL NOTES

Taking a trip abroad? Don't forget your sketchbook! Exotic locations, fresh faces, new experiences – all will bring excitement and energy to your work. Stroll around and take in the sights, the smells, and the atmosphere. A small hardback sketchbook can be pulled out quickly when something catches your eye, and you can tuck yourself into a doorway to avoid the attentions of curious onlookers. Keep your sketches small; you can draw with a spontaneity that is difficult to achieve on a larger scale. Just draw what you see and don't worry about the results. Learn to simplify the forms and identify the telling details that sum up the liveliness and atmosphere of the place.

Collect interesting little items that are reminders of the places you visit.

✳ COLORED pencils and
felt-tips are a quick and
convenient way to capture
the color and atmosphere
of an exotic location.

CAFÉ SOCIETY

Restaurants, bars, and cafés are great places for sketching unusual characters and expressive poses and gestures. Look for shapes, patterns, and colors, too, in the structure of the room, the network of tables and chairs, and the table settings. Find a quiet corner and hide behind a newspaper and a cup of coffee — you don't want your subjects to notice what you are up to!

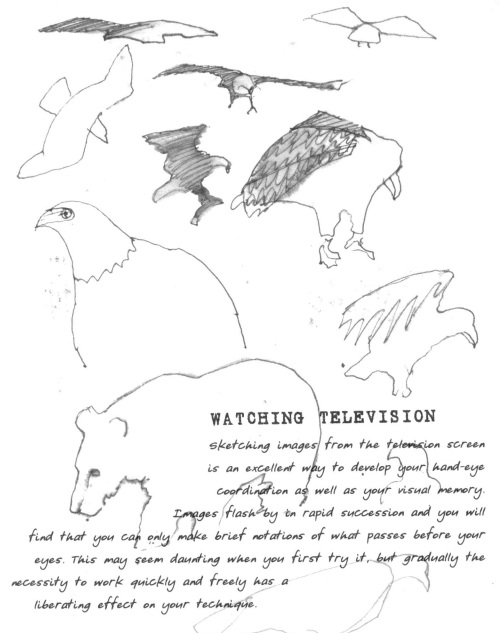

WATCHING TELEVISION

Sketching images from the television screen is an excellent way to develop your hand-eye coordination as well as your visual memory. Images flash by in rapid succession and you will find that you can only make brief notations of what passes before your eyes. This may seem daunting when you first try it, but gradually the necessity to work quickly and freely has a liberating effect on your technique.

* THE best television
programs to draw from
are those that show
repeated moving
images, such as
wildlife documentaries
and sports events.

Let your brain and hand respond rapidly and intuitively to what you see.

"Still Life of Fruit" (1913)
ILYA IVANOVICH MASHKOV
(1881-1994).

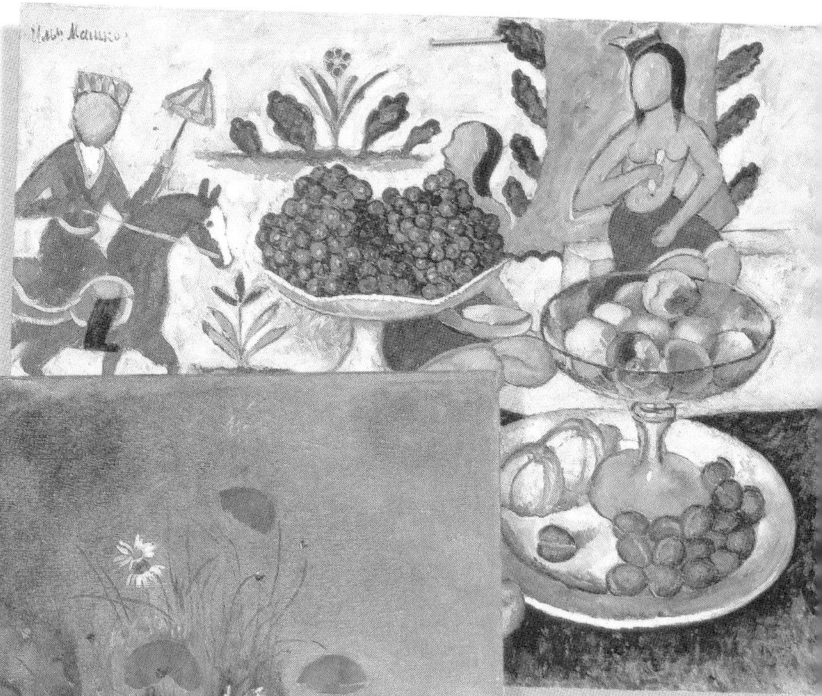

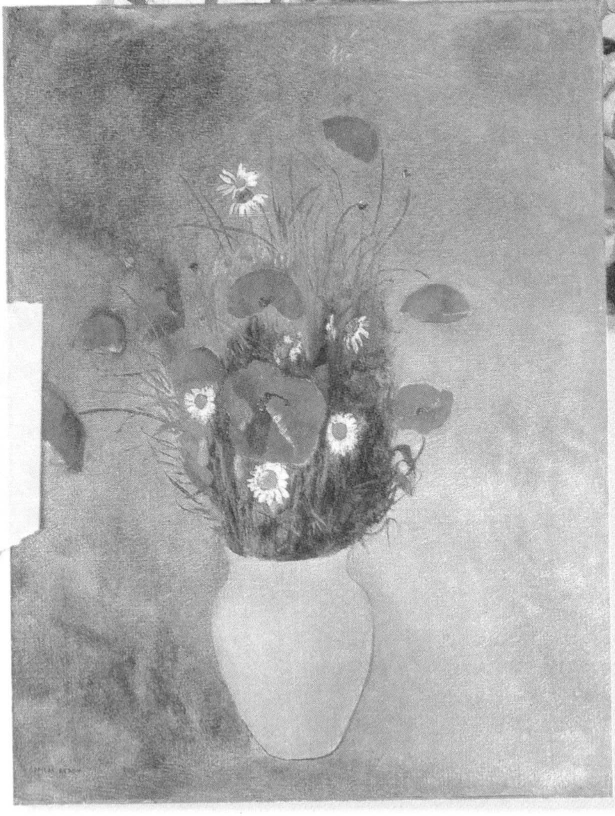

"Red Poppies and
Ox-eye Daisies"
(ca. 1913)
ODILON REDON
(1840-1916).

"Still Life of Raspberries, Gooseberries, Peach, and Plums on a Mossy Bank" OLIVER CLARE (1853-1927).

NATURE STUDIES

Nature provides a limitless source of subjects for sketching. You can study natural subjects outdoors - waves and reflections in water, a stand of trees, a group of clouds, a patch of wildflowers. Or you can work at home using objects gathered outdoors such as leaves, grasses and flowers, pine cones, seedheads, shells, and so on.

NATURAL SHAPES

The breathtaking variety of shapes, textures, patterns, and colors that can be found in nature offers plenty of scope for creative interpretation in sketchbook drawings. It can be absorbing and instructive to interpret the particular qualities of a natural object such as a stone, a leaf, or an insect through the character of the medium you use and the marks you make with it. A sweep of charcoal or pastel over rough paper, for instance, mimics the rough texture of stone and gnarled wood, while the silvery lead of a hard pencil will describe the graceful curve of a feather.

✳ BOTANICAL illustrations can be a starting-off point for creative interpretations of natural forms.

Pick out interesting details that simply fascinate in themselves.

※ THE thin, scratchy
lines made by a dip
pen and ink search
out the intricacies
of a gnarled and
twisted section of a
bramble hedge.

FLOWERS AND PLANTS

You can easily fill an entire sketchbook with studies of individual flowers, leaves, stems, buds, and seedheads. Flowers are fragile and yet highly structured. Start by sketching in the main shapes, breaking them down into simple geometric forms. Daisies, pansies, and sunflowers are basically circles and ellipses; tulips and lilies are cups and cones; roses and chrysanthemums are balls or spheres. Try to ignore the attraction of color and texture and concentrate first on form and structure. Look for the rhythms that give a sense of growth. Half-close your eyes to see the play of light and shade on the leaves and petals.

* LOOK for the patterns of light and shade that help to describe form.

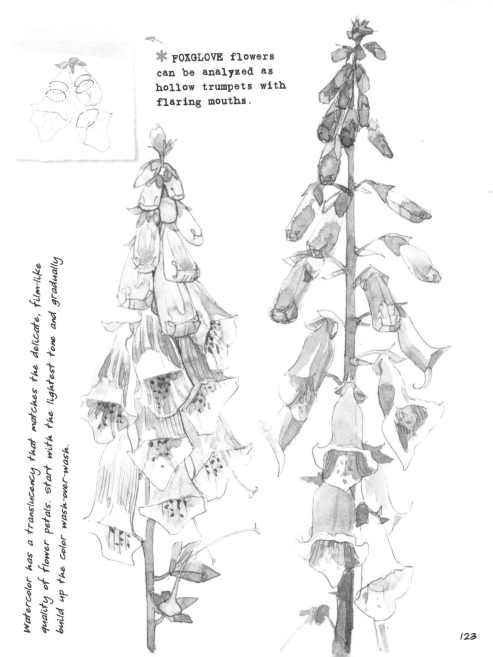

✳ FOXGLOVE flowers
can be analyzed as
hollow trumpets with
flaring mouths.

Watercolor has a translucency that matches the delicate, film-like quality of flower petals. Start with the lightest tone and gradually build up the color wash-over-wash.

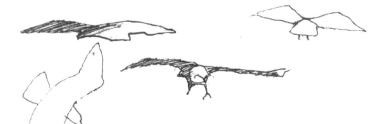

ANIMALS IN ACTION

Capturing the grace and agility of a moving animal is difficult but rewarding. Start off by drawing animals in a zoo or in a field. Here the animals are moving but because they are in a confined space their gestures are fairly regular and repetitive. This means you can wait for a limb to adopt a similar position perhaps several times, each occasion giving you the chance to refine and correct your drawing.

Look for the position of the legs and where the weight is carried.

The tail accentuates the rhythm of the animal's body.

Photographs will give you a good insight into an animal's characteristic movements. These are from the famous series of microsecond stills of animals in motion taken by Eadweard Muybridge.

TIP

When drawing a moving animal you have to work quickly, so choose your medium accordingly. Soft pencil, graphite stick, charcoal, brush and ink, felt-tip, and crayon are all ideal because they travel freely over the paper and help you sketch your impressions quickly.

Make the drawing itself convey a feeling of movement. Don't fix the animal on the paper but give it an indistinct outline, or perhaps several outlines, to show that it is not static. Sweeping, gestural marks, drawn with great speed, imply action. Movement can also be suggested by softening or fading out the parts, such as the legs, that are moving.

125

BEACHCOMBING

The seashore is a treasure trove of fascinating natural objects. Bring home pebbles, shells, starfish, pieces of seaweed, and any other bits of flotsam and jetsam you find in order to study them in detail at your leisure and make exploratory drawings. Think of them as working drawings, not necessarily finished pictures. Use them as reference material in the same way you might use magazine cuttings and photographs.

Use natural objects as a basis for a sketch then customize it with your own style.

PRACTICE

Assemble a group of natural objects that present a variety of contrasting shapes, patterns, and textures. Make a series of studies of the group, using different drawing media on textured and colored papers. Try to find ways of describing the surface qualities and contrasting one with another.

NATURE
IN CLOSEUP

A closer view of natural forms reveals a rich variety of colors, textures, and patterns that can be explored for their own sake. Try cutting some fruits and vegetables in half. Cabbages, cauliflowers, peppers, tomatoes, and pomegranates, for instance, all reveal interesting cross-sections to draw. You can have great fun creating stylized or abstract designs based on these patterns.

＊ USE inks, watercolors, and soft pastels to express the exuberant colors of nature.

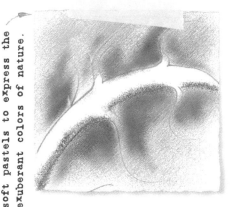

CABBAGE COLOR PALETTE

PRACTICE

Cut a red cabbage in half and make a larger-than-life study of the patterns within. Use a color medium such as pastel, conté, or colored pencil and try to interpret creatively the compact, compressed forms of its furled leaves and the pattern of the swirling lines.

Crop in on your subject and
let it fill a whole page.
Seen from an unexpected
viewpoint, even humble
cabbages can make a
striking image.

In the winter, use charcoal or fiber-tip pen to emphasize the harsh, linear rhythms of leafless trees and the stark tracery of twigs and branches.

If you are sketching in color, observe what type of green the foliage is — whether dark or light, warm or cool.

* JUST like people, each tree has its own individual character and "gesture."

sketch individual leaves as the seasons change.

TREES Make sketches of individual trees in all seasons and watch the change from the skeletal winter outline through to the abundant green masses of summer foliage. Before you start to draw a tree, first look for the main shapes and masses. Compare the height of the tree to the spread of its branches and try to get the proportions right. Try to draw the trunk and branches with the same kind of searching sensitivity you would employ for a figure drawing.

"The Sleep of Reason Produces Monsters" (1799)
FRANCISCO DE GOYA (1746-1828).

"Phaethon" ODILON REDON (1840-1916).

SKETCHING FROM IMAGINATION

Your sketchbook is the perfect playground in which to let loose your imagination. Without the pressures of producing a "proper" picture, you are free to experiment with ideas and techniques, indulge in creative daydreaming, and record your private thoughts and observations.

WORKING FROM MEMORY

We've all experienced how certain smells can trigger long-forgotten memories. In the same way, a sketch can act as a trigger or reminder of a scene. The sketch may be a mere scribble or fragment, but the very act of drawing something means you have really studied it and it will be "imprinted" in your mind's eye. Thus a few lines and color notes, along with your visual memory, are all you need to recreate a vivid impression of the scene. When you are making reference sketches for paintings, try to ignore unnecessary details and focus quickly on the essential elements. Look for the key colors, tones, or shapes that seem to encapsulate the character or atmosphere of the subject.

* "MEMENTOS" such as pebbles, shells, feathers, and leaves picked up while out walking can trigger memories of a particular place and also make interesting drawing subjects in themselves.

It is clear what this watercolor sketch represents but there is no attempt at detailed description. It is more about atmosphere and mood.

CREATIVE PLAY

Do you ever get "artist's block"? You're in the mood to draw, but haven't a clue what to draw? Simply start with no specific subject in mind and doodle on a large sheet of paper until you see something emerging that activates your imagination and suggests an image. We've all, as children, made pictures out of ink blots. This idea of creating a picture out of random shapes goes back to Leonardo da Vinci, who urged artists to discover images by studying the patterns of stained walls, moving clouds, or the dying embers of a fire. In the 18th century, Alexander Cozens invented a system of "blot drawings"; he scattered ink blots randomly onto paper to produce a series of accidental shapes from which he created images of landscapes and other compositions.

Children can create fantastical figures from simple doodles.

Try dripping some ink onto paper from the end of a paintbrush. Study the random pattern made until a visual image comes to mind — perhaps a landscape or a stormy sea. Develop the image by adding drawn lines over the printed marks. The effects can be varied by dripping ink onto dry or wet paper.

Most of us doodle when we're on the phone or stuck in a boring meeting. Doodling is a way to think things out, to solve problems, to get in touch with our inner thoughts. Doodles done on scraps of paper have a directness and rhythm that may be missing in our "serious" work.

"Look at the spots on the wall, at the ashes of the hearth, at the clouds, or in the gutter: on careful observation, you will make wonderful discoveries there." Leonardo da Vinci, "Treatise on Painting."

FLIGHTS OF FANCY

Imagination is a
powerful faculty.
A child's imaginary
world is as genuine
to him or her as
the "real" one, and even
as adults we daydream.
Through drawing, it is
possible to tap directly into
the imagination and explore an
inner world. Sketch the
inside of your mind.
Draw fantastic beasts,
wild and wacky cars, a
Martian landscape. Distort
shapes, play visual games
with perspective and scale.
Play with illusion and space
and the idea of seeing subjects
in unexpected ways. Follow your
instincts and intuitions, try out ideas
and enjoy drawing for its own sake.

Be inspired by Paul Klee and "take a line for a walk." With no attempt at conscious planning, draw lines on the page that eventually suggest a real or fantastic subject from your imagination. Let your pencil or pen record the free movements of your hand, your gestures guided by your subconscious. If you like, you can then go on to develop the image in more detail in another drawing.

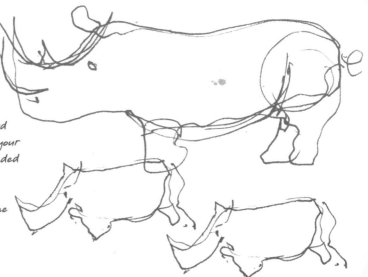

LEARNING FROM THE MASTERS Since the Renaissance, artists have learned by studying and copying from works by past masters. Many galleries and museums have artists' sketchbooks and drawings on display. Take a sketchbook along and make drawings from works that appeal to you, or copy from reproductions in art books. The idea is not to labor over an exact copy of the work; look upon it as a process of investigation and discovery. You'll find that it provides valuable insights into the artist's personal "handwriting" and use of color, line, and composition.

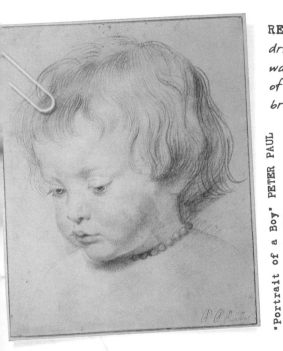

"Portrait of a Boy" PETER PAUL RUBENS (1577-1640).

REMBRANDT One of the greatest draftsmen of all time, Rembrandt was fascinated by the effects of light on form. Using pen, brush, and ink, he was able to convey intense emotion with a few telling lines.

RUBENS Rubens was a master at handling lights and darks to create the illusion of volume. He produced extraordinarily sensitive sketches using finely hatched strokes.

VAN GOGH *As with his paintings, van Gogh's drawings, made with a reed pen, are full of expressive marks: rapid hatchings, swirling curlicues, waves, and stipple dots.*

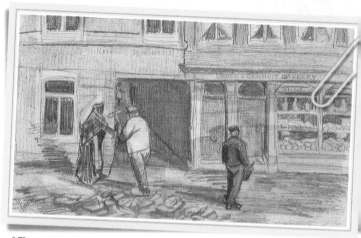

"The Bakery in de Geest" VINCENT VAN GOGH (1853-90).

TURNER *Turner's innumerable watercolor sketches demonstrate his ability to condense the essentials of a scene into a few rapid strokes.*

CONSTABLE *Throughout his life, Constable made studies outdoors in pencil and watercolor, recording the changing effects of weather and time of day with a wonderful freshness and immediacy.*

"Landscape with Trees and a Distant Mansion" JOHN CONSTABLE (1776-1837).

INDEX

ACKNOWLEDGMENTS

The publisher would like to thank the following for the use of pictures:

✳ Academia, Venice: 76B.

✳ The Bridgeman Art Library, London: 22T (Fitzwilliam Museum, Cambridge); 22B (Potteries Museum and Art Gallery, Stoke-on-Trent); 23T (Galerie Daniel Malingue); 34T (Leamington Spa Art Gallery); 34B (Stapleton Collection); 46T (Harris Museum and Art Gallery, Preston); 46BL (Offentliche Kunstsammlung, Basel); 47T (Castle Museum and Art Gallery, Nottingham); 76TL (Gavin Graham Gallery); 76B, 85T, 100B, 111T, 119T (Private Collection); 81B (Scottish National Portrait Gallery); 84T (Ashmolean Museum, Oxford); 84B (The Fine Art Society); 110, 141T (Haags Gemeente Museum, Netherlands); 118T (Radichtev Museum Saratova); 118B (Phillips Fine Art Auctioneers); 133T (Louvre, Paris); 140 (Graphische Sammlung, Albertine, Vienna); 141B (Victoria and Albert Museum, London).

✳ BAL / Christies, London: 100T, 101T; BAL/Giraudon: 77T (Musée d'Orsay, Paris).

✳ Corbis, London: 35T (By Kind permission of the Trustees of the National Gallery, London), 42 (Francis G. Mayer), 58L (Bettman), 59T (Kimbel Art Museum), 132 (Archivo Iconograpahico, S.A.).

✳ Hulton Getty, London: 54BR.

✳ Eadweard Muybridge: 125T.

"Drawing sketches is like planting seeds in order to get pictures later."

VINCENT VAN GOGH